P9-CDK-547

BE A SCIENTIST
LET'S INVESTIGATE FORCES

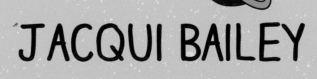

JACQUI BAILEY

CRABTREE
PUBLISHING COMPANY
WWW.CRABTREEBOOKS.COM

CRABTREE
PUBLISHING COMPANY
WWW.CRABTREEBOOKS.COM

Author: Jacqui Bailey

Editorial director: Kathy Middleton

Series editor: Julia Bird

Editor: Ellen Rodger

Illustrator: Ed Myer

Packaged by: Collaborate

Proofreader: Petrice Custance

**Production coordinator
and Prepress technician:** Ken Wright

Print coordinator: Katherine Berti

Library and Achives Canada Cataloguing in Publication

Title: Let's investigate forces / Jacqui Bailey.
Other titles: Investigating forces
Names: Bailey, Jacqui, author.
Description: Series statement: Be a scientist |
  Previously published under title: Investigating forces. |
  Includes index.
Identifiers: Canadiana (print) 20200353950 |
  Canadiana (ebook) 20200354019 |
  ISBN 9781427127723 (hardcover) |
  ISBN 9781427127785 (softcover) |
  ISBN 9781427127846 (HTML)
Subjects: LCSH: Force and energy—Juvenile literature. |
  LCSH: Force and energy—Experiments—Juvenile literature. |
  LCSH: Mechanics—Juvenile literature. | LCSH: Mechanics—
  Experiments—Juvenile literature.
Classification: LCC QC73.4 .B35 2021 | DDC j531/.6—dc23

Library of Congress Cataloging-in-Publication Data

Names: Bailey, Jacqui, author.
Title: Let's investigate forces / Jacqui Bailey.
Description: New York, NY : Crabtree Publishing Company, 2021. |
  Series: Be a scientist | Includes index.
Identifiers: LCCN 2020045062 (print) | LCCN 2020045063 (ebook) |
  ISBN 9781427127723 (hardcover) |
  ISBN 9781427127785 (paperback) |
  ISBN 9781427127846 (ebook)
Subjects: LCSH: Force and energy--Juvenile literature.
Classification: LCC QC73.4 .B347 2021 (print) | LCC QC73.4 (ebook) |
  DDC 531/.6--dc23
LC record available at https://lccn.loc.gov/2020045062
LC ebook record available at https://lccn.loc.gov/2020045063

Crabtree Publishing Company
www.crabtreebooks.com   1–800–387–7650
Published in 2021 by Crabtree Publishing Company

First published in Great Britain in 2019 by Wayland
Copyright © Hodder & Stoughton, 2019

All rights reserved. No part of this publication may be
reproduced, stored in a retrieval system or be transmitted
in any form or by any means, electronic, mechanical,
photocopying, recording, or otherwise, without the prior
written permission of the copyright owner.

The text in this book was previously published
in the series 'Investigating Science'

Printed in the U.S.A./122020/CG20201014

Every attempt has been made to clear copyright.
Should there be any inadvertent omission please apply
to the publisher for rectification.

Published in Canada
Crabtree Publishing
616 Welland Ave.
St. Catharines, Ontario
L2M 5V6

Published in the United States
Crabtree Publishing
347 Fifth Avenue
Suite 1402–145
New York, NY 10016

BE A SCIENTIST

LET'S INVESTIGATE FORCES

CRABTREE
PUBLISHING COMPANY
WWW.CRABTREEBOOKS.COM

CONTENTS

ON THE MOVE

Look around you.
What can you see that moves?

YOU WILL NEED
A sheet of paper
A pencil and a ruler
Space to jump around in!

THINK about all the different ways things move.

· Balls bounce, marbles roll, cars race, windmills whirl, and cranes lift.

· Animals stretch, run, climb, crawl, swim, fly, hop, and wiggle.

What about you? How many **movements** can you make?

walk
bend
run
twist
jump

HOW MANY WAYS CAN YOU MOVE?

1 Use the pencil and ruler to draw a line down the middle of the paper.

2 In the left-hand column, list all the different movements you can think of.

"BECAUSE...

We can move in so many ways because of the **joints** and **muscles** in our bodies. Joints link our bones together like hinges. Muscles pull on the bones and make them move at the joints. Our muscles are using a **force** to make us move.

"

4 Now see what movements your friends can make.

3 Try to do all the movements on your list. In the right-hand column, tick off each one as you do it.

PUSH AND PULL

Everything needs a force to make it move. Although you cannot see a force, you can see what it does. A force is either a push or a pull.

THINK about what happens when you push or pull something.

· You pull open a drawer.

· You push away a soccer ball with a kick.

· You lift a wheelbarrow with a pull, and then push it along.

Try moving some other things. Do you use pushes or pulls?

YOU WILL NEED

A sheet of paper
A pencil and a ruler
A group of objects
(e.g. a toy car, a bouncy ball, a roll of tape, a marble, an eraser, a drink with a straw in it, a pencil)

HOW DO YOU MAKE THINGS MOVE?

1 Divide your paper into two columns with a line down the middle.

2 Write the word push at the top of one column and pull at the top of the other.

3 Look at your objects and think about the best way to move each one with a push or a pull. Write the name of the object in the column with that heading.

4 Now make the objects move and find out if you were right.

" BECAUSE...

All of the objects move because of a push or a pull. Pushing something moves it away from you, pulling something moves it toward you. For example, sucking a drink through a straw pulls the liquid toward your mouth. "

BIG PUSH, LITTLE PUSH

We can make things move with a big force or a small one.

THINK about what happens when you push a friend on a swing.

· A small push makes the swing move a little.

· A big push makes the swing move a lot.

Try pushing some coins to find out how the strength of a force changes the way an object moves.

YOU WILL NEED

A large piece of paper, about 12 inches (30.5 cm) wide by 18 inches (46 cm) long

A pencil and a ruler

A large board or tabletop

Tape

3 coins of the same size

WHICH FORCE MOVES A COIN THE MOST?

1 Use the ruler to mark every 4 inches (10 cm) down both sides of the sheet of paper. Draw lines to connect each pair of marks and number each line.

2 Lay the paper flat on the board or tabletop, so its top end lies along one edge. Tape it firmly in position.

3 Place a coin on the top edge of the paper so it juts out a little over the side.

4 Give the coin a shove with your hand. How far can you make it slide along the paper? What happens if you hit the next coin harder, or less hard?

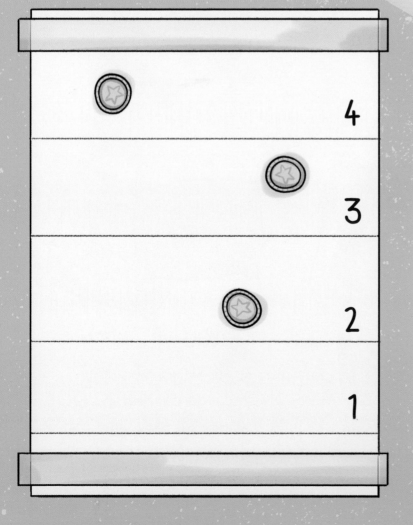

" BECAUSE...

A big push makes a coin travel further than a small push. This is because the greater the force used on an object, the more it moves. The same is true of pulling. You can see how this works when you pull on an **elastic** band. **"**

HEAVY AND LIGHT

A light object is easy to move. It can be hard to move a heavy object.

THINK about the amount of force you need to move a heavy object or a light one.

· Can you throw a basketball as far as you can throw a tennis ball? Does it take more or less force?

· Is it easier to move a chair or a table? Which is heavier?

Investigate how much force you use to move a box.

YOU WILL NEED

2 strips of paper
A large cardboard box
A pile of soft cushions
A pile of books

WHICH BOX TAKES THE MOST FORCE TO MOVE?

1 Put the strips of paper on the floor about 10 feet (3 m) apart, to make a start and a finish line.

2 Put the empty box in front of one line and push or pull it to the other line. How much force did you need to use?

3 Fill the cardboard box with cushions and push or pull it back to the start line. Was it easier or harder this time?

4 Now fill the box with books. How much force does it take to push or pull it between the lines? (If you cannot move the box at all, take out books until you can!)

" BECAUSE...

The box of books took the most force to move because it was much heavier than the box of cushions. A light object needs less force to make it move than a heavy one. "

13

CRASH!

When a moving object hits something that is not moving, a force passes from one object to the other.

THINK about how the game of bowling is played.
- You roll a ball at some pins and try to knock them over.

Does the weight of the bowling ball matter?

What happens if you roll the ball quickly or more slowly?

YOU WILL NEED
4 small plastic bottles
Some water
A strip of paper
A tennis ball
A sponge ball the same size as the tennis ball

WHAT MAKES THE BOTTLES FALL?

1 Fill each bottle half way with water. These are your pins.

2 Line up the pins on a flat surface and walk five big strides away. Mark this point with the strip of paper. Always stand behind this line to bowl.

3 Roll the tennis ball at each pin in turn and try to knock it over.

4 Now use the sponge ball instead, rolling it at the same speed as the tennis ball. What is the difference?

5 Try again with each ball, this time rolling them faster.

" BECAUSE...

The tennis ball is much better at knocking over the bottles than the sponge ball. This is because when a heavy moving object hits something, it does so with a greater force than a light object moving at the same speed. "

THINK about what would happen if you were in the way of a fast-moving car.
· If the car hit you, the force of its movement would knock you over and could even kill you.

15

CHANGE DIRECTION

A force can make a moving object change direction.

THINK about how you ride a bicycle.

• You use a force to turn the handlebars.
• The bicycle changes direction. How can you make a moving ball change direction?

YOU WILL NEED
A soft ball
A bat or a racket
A long piece of string, about 6.5 feet (2 m)
Tape
A long pole, such as. a broom handle

WHAT MAKES A MOVING BALL CHANGE DIRECTION?

1 Start by hitting the ball with the bat and watch how the ball moves.

2 Now tie one end of the string tightly around the ball, as shown.

3 Tie the other end of the string to one end of the pole and tape it in place.

4 Push the other end of the pole firmly into the ground (you might need an adult to help you).

5 Now hit the ball again. What happens this time?

THINK about the ball games that you play. What forces do you use to change the direction of the ball?

" **BECAUSE...**

The ball will travel in a straight line until it reaches the end of the string. Then, the force of the string pulling against the moving ball will tug it to one side. "

17

STRETCH AND SQUASH

A force can change something's shape. A pushing force can squash it, and a pulling force can stretch it.

YOU WILL NEED

Some modeling clay

A pencil and paper

A collection of other materials (e.g. a sponge, a rubber band, plastic wrap, a piece of paper, a block of wood, a soda can, an empty plastic bottle)

THINK about what happens when you use your hands to change the shape of something.

twist

squeeze

HOW CAN YOU CHANGE SOMETHING'S SHAPE?

1 Take some modeling clay and make it into different shapes. Think about the actions you used, such as twist, roll, stretch, or squeeze.

2 List each action. Write next to it if it was a pushing action, a pulling action, or both.

3 Try stretching or squashing the other materials you have collected.

4 Make a list of the materials and how you changed their shape, if at all. Make a note of what happened when you let them go.

" BECAUSE...

The shape of a material changes because it is being pushed together or pulled apart. Some things need more force than others to make them change shape. Modeling clay, for example, needs only a small force to change shape, but stretching plastic wrap requires a stronger force. Changing the shape of a block of wood needs a much stronger force than using our hands alone.

Some materials are bendable and spring back into shape when you let them go. We say they are elastic. Elastic materials have a force of their own that brings them back to their original shape when the outside force stops pushing or pulling them. "

19

NATURAL FORCES

There are forces in nature that make things move.

YOU WILL NEED

A large square of stiff paper or thin cardboard, about 6 square inches (15.2 sq cm)

A pencil, a ruler, and scissors, 2 small beads

A long pin with a bobble on the end

A small wooden stick (e.g. a dowling rod or a pencil)

A small hammer

An adult to help you

THINK about things that move without people pushing or pulling them.
· A flag on a flagpole flaps.
· Kites swoop around the sky.
What makes them move?

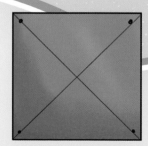

WHAT MAKES A PINWHEEL WHIRL?

1. Draw two lines to divide your paper into triangles, as shown. Make a dot on the lines just inside each corner.

2. Inside each triangle, draw a dotted line 0.5 inches (1.25 cm) to the right of a corner to 0.5 inches (1.25 cm) short of the middle. Cut along these lines.

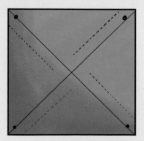

3 Without creasing the paper, carefully bend each corner into the center so that the corner dots are on top of one another.

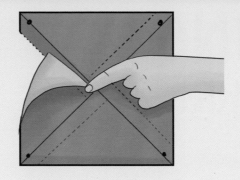

4 Ask an adult to help you thread one bead onto the pin. Push the pin through the dots, and then thread the second bead onto the pin on the other side.

5 Now push the pin into one end of the wooden stick. Your helper may need to tap it in with a hammer. Your pinwheel should move easily if you push it with your finger.

6 What happens when you take your pinwheel outside and hold it up to the wind? What happens if you blow on it?

" BECAUSE...

Your pinwheel whirls around because the wind pushes air into its sails and makes the wheel spin. Wind can be a very powerful force— think of **hurricane's** strong winds!

"

SLIPPING AND STICKING

Forces make things move, but they can also slow things down. **Friction** is a force that slows things down.

YOU WILL NEED
A small, smooth wooden plank
A test object, such as a wooden block
A pile of books
3 different test surfaces, such as felt, sandpaper, or shiny plastic
Tape
A pencil and paper

THINK about how things slide across different surfaces.

· Sliding down a slide is easy and fast.

· Sliding down a grassy hill is slow and difficult.

What is the difference between the two surfaces?

WHAT DIFFERENCE DOES A SURFACE MAKE?

1 Place your test object at one end of the plank. Raise that end until the object starts to slide. Prop up the plank at that angle with some books.

2 Tape each of your test surfaces onto the plank in turn. How does your test object slide on each surface? Do you have to raise the plank higher?

3 List the surfaces you use, including the wooden surface, and mark them out of four (one for the smoothest and four for the roughest). Now mark them out of four for slipperiness. How do their marks compare?

" BECAUSE...

The smoothest material is also the most slippery. This is because a rough surface produces more friction. Friction is what happens when one object rubs against another. Friction slows things down and stops them from sliding. "

THINK about what would happen without friction. Every surface would be as slippery as ice.

• How would we walk?

• How would we turn a door handle?

FIGHTING FORCE

Like friction, both air and water push against moving objects and slow them down. This is called **resistance.**

THINK about the ways in which air or water push against you.

- When you paddle in a swimming pool, you feel the water pushing against your body.
- When you walk with your jacket open, you feel air pushing against you. The air is resisting your movement.

How can air and water resistance be useful?

YOU WILL NEED

A plastic bag
Scissors
Thin string or strong thread
2 identical plastic toy figures
A stopwatch or clock

HOW DOES AIR RESISTANCE WORK?

1 Cut a large square out of the plastic bag.

2 Cut four pieces of string, each about 11 inches (28 cm) long.

"BECAUSE...

The toy with the parachute takes longer to reach the ground because, as it falls, air is trapped underneath the parachute. This air pushes upward against the parachute and the resistance slows down the toy's fall.

"

5 Stand on a sturdy chair, but be careful! First, drop the toy that doesn't have a parachute and time how long it takes to reach the ground.

4 Twist the other ends of string together and then tie them around one of the toy figures.

6 Now drop the toy with the parachute and count again. Which one takes longer to fall?

3 Make a tiny hole in each corner of the plastic square, about 0.5 inches (1.25 cm) from the edge. Tie a piece of string in each hole in the plastic.

ALL FALL DOWN

Things fall toward the ground because of a force called **gravity**. Gravity pulls everything toward the center of the Earth. Without it, we would all float away into space.

THINK about how gravity pulls things downward.

• When you drop a book, it falls to the ground.

• However high you throw a ball, it always falls back to Earth. But other forces also affect the pull of gravity on an object.

Think about the parachute test on pages 24-25, then try this one.

YOU WILL NEED
2 sheets of paper
A tennis ball

HOW DOES SHAPE AFFECT GRAVITY?

1 Crumple one sheet of paper into a fairly tight ball. It should be about the same size as the tennis ball.

2 Carefully stand on a chair or table, with an adult to spot you. Hold both balls as high as you can. Let them go at exactly the same moment. Which one reaches the ground first?

3 Now, hold the other sheet of paper flat in one hand and the paper ball in the other. Drop them both together. What happens this time?

" BECAUSE...

The two balls hit the ground at the same time. This is because the pull of gravity is the same on both objects. The flat sheet of paper falls more slowly than the paper ball. This is because the flat paper has a bigger surface so there is more air resistance to slow it down.

"

GLOSSARY

Elastic

materials stretch and become longer when you pull them. They snap back into their original shape when you let go.

Forces

make things move, slow down, or change direction. They push or pull on things. You cannot see a force, but you can see what it does and feel how strong it is.

Friction

is a force that slows things down. It happens when two surfaces rub together. Rough surfaces create more friction than smooth surfaces. Friction allows us to grip and hold onto things. Without it, everything would be slippery.

Gravity

is a pulling force. On Earth, gravity is the force that pulls everything toward Earth's center. This is why things always fall downward.

Hurricanes

are powerful winds that whirl around in a gigantic circle. They often bring torrential rain and whip up huge waves at sea. Hurricane winds can blow at speeds of more than 200 miles per hour (320 kph), and can lift cars and flatten houses.

Joints

are like the hinges on a door. They link our bones together and allow our arms, legs, and other body parts to bend.

A dolphin's sleek shape helps it cut through, or resist, the force of water.

Materials

can be hard, such as metal, or soft, such as jelly. They can be invisible, such as the air we breathe. Everything in the universe is made of some kind of material.

Movement

is what happens when something changes its position in some way. Movements can be big, such as an aircraft taking off, or very small, such as the blink of an eye.

Muscles

are the parts of your body that pull on your bones and make them move at the joints. You have more than 600 muscles in your body.

Resistance

is what happens when a force pushes or pulls against an object and slows it down. Air and water push against objects moving through them. The faster an object moves, the more air or water will resist it.

When two things rub together, the friction between them makes heat. Try rubbing your hands together and feel how friction makes them feel hot.

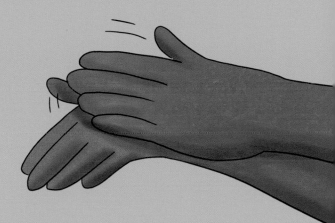

The pull of gravity gives things weight. The Moon has gravity too, but it is smaller than Earth so its gravity is weaker. Things weigh less on the Moon than they do on Earth.

LEARNING MORE

BOOKS

Boothroyd, Jennifer. *Give it a Push! Give it a Pull! A Look at Forces.* Lerner Publishing Group, 2010.

Claybourne, Anna. *Recreate Discoveries About Forces.* Crabtree Publishing, 2019.

Spilsbury, Richard. *Investigating Forces and Motion.* Crabtree Publishing, 2018.

WEBSITES

Learn more about forces and motion at:.
www.dkfindout.com/us/science/forces-and-motion/

Visit this site for some fun forces and motion games:
https://sciencetrek.org/sciencetrek/topics/force_and_motion/games.cm

PLACES TO VISIT

The Sciencenter in Ithaca, New York, started as a volunteer-run science program at a local school and has grown to serve more than a million guests through its online programs. Check out its virtual programs at: www.sciencenter.org/programs.html.

NOTE TO PARENTS AND TEACHERS:

Every effort has been made by the publisher to ensure that these websites contain no inappropriate or offensive material. However, because of the nature of the Internet, it is impossible to guarantee that the content of these sites will not be altered. We strongly recommend that Internet access is supervised by a responsible adult.

INDEX